Captain
Bill Pinkney's
Journey

a Collections for Young Scholars book

WRITTEN BY

BILL
PINKNEY

ILLUSTRATED BY

JAN
ADKINS

OPEN COURT PUBLISHING COMPANY

CHICAGO AND PERU, ILLINOIS

PROGRAM AUTHORS
Marilyn Jager Adams
Carl Bereiter
Jan Hirshberg
Valerie Anderson
S. A. Bernier

CONSULTING AUTHORS
Michael Pressley
Marsha Roit
Iva Carruthers
Bill Pinkney

CHAIRMAN
M. Blouke Carus

PRESIDENT
André W. Carus

EDUCATION DIRECTOR
Carl Bereiter

CONCEPT
Barbara Conteh

EXECUTIVE EDITOR
Shirley Graudin

EDITOR
Charis Wahl

ART DIRECTOR
John Grandits

VICE-PRESIDENT, PRODUCTION
AND MANUFACTURING
Chris Vancalbergh

PERMISSIONS COORDINATOR
Diane Sikora

ILLUSTRATOR
Jan Adkins

This book was designed by Inkfish Design Studio. Jan Adkins's illustrations and maps were done in pencil and acrylic on linen board or electronically. Composition and electronic page makeup were provided by Brian Jones.

Printed in the United States of America

ISBN 0-8126-0248-X

10 9 8 7 6 5 4 3 2

ACKNOWLEDGMENTS (PHOTOGRAPHY)

cover/© Scott Coe
5   © Mush Emmons
6/7 Boston Harbor/© Steve Elmore, Tom Stack Associates
7   Commitment/© Mush Emmons
12   Pilot whales/© Doug Perrine, DRK Photo
13   Bermuda/© Roderick Beebe
16   Street band/© Mush Emmons
17   Macaw/© Leonard Lee Rue III, DRK Photo
17   Rain forest/© Michael Fogdei, DRK Photo
19   Bill on radio/© Bill Pinkney
20   Commitment/© Mush Emmons
21   Lion/© Jeremy Woodhouse, DRK Photo
21   Rhinoceros/© Kennan Ward, DRK Photo
21   South African family/© Bill Pinkney
23   Storm/© Bill Pinkney
24   Tasmanian devil/© Bill Pinkney
25   Kangaroo/© Stephen J. Krasemann, DRK Photo
25   Koala/© John Cancalosi, DRK Photo
25   Kookaburra/© Stephen J. Krasemann, DRK Photo
26   Bird/© Bill Pinkney
26   Hawksbill turtle/© Doug Perrine, DRK Photo
28   Cape Horn/© Wolfgang Kaehler
30   Commitment/© Scott Coe
30   Bill Pinkney/© Scott Coe
31   Celebration/© Scott Coe

SAILING CALENDAR

Left	Sailing Days	Arrived
Boston, Massachusetts August 5, 1990	8	Bermuda August 13, 1990
Bermuda August 21, 1990	53	Salvador, Brazil October 13, 1990
Salvador, Brazil November 9, 1990	34	Cape Town, South Africa December 13, 1990
Cape Town, South Africa January 11, 1991	56	Hobart, Australia March 8, 1991

Captain Bill stayed in Hobart, waiting for Australia's summer before setting sail again.

Left	Sailing Days	Arrived
Hobart, Australia December 24, 1991	63	Punta del Este, Uruguay February 25, 1992
Punta del Este, Uruguay April 6, 1992	10	Salvador, Brazil April 16, 1992
Salvador, Brazil April 24, 1992	27	Bermuda May 21, 1992
Bermuda June 1, 1992	8	Boston, Massachusetts June 9, 1992

A ship's clock

 When I was a boy, I dreamed about boats, so I started reading about boats.

"I will grow up to be Captain Bill," I said, "and sail across wide oceans."

I made a commitment—that's a powerful promise—to sail around the world in my own boat.

When I grew up, I learned to sail. I read more about boats. I learned to use tools and fix equipment. I learned to use radios and radar. I studied geography and weather.

I learned enough to be captain of my own boat. Today I leave from Boston to sail around the world!

I have said good-bye to dozens of Boston schoolchildren. They will talk with me by radio when I am at sea.

Boston Harbor

Captain Bill named his boat <u>Commitment</u> for his powerful promise.

7

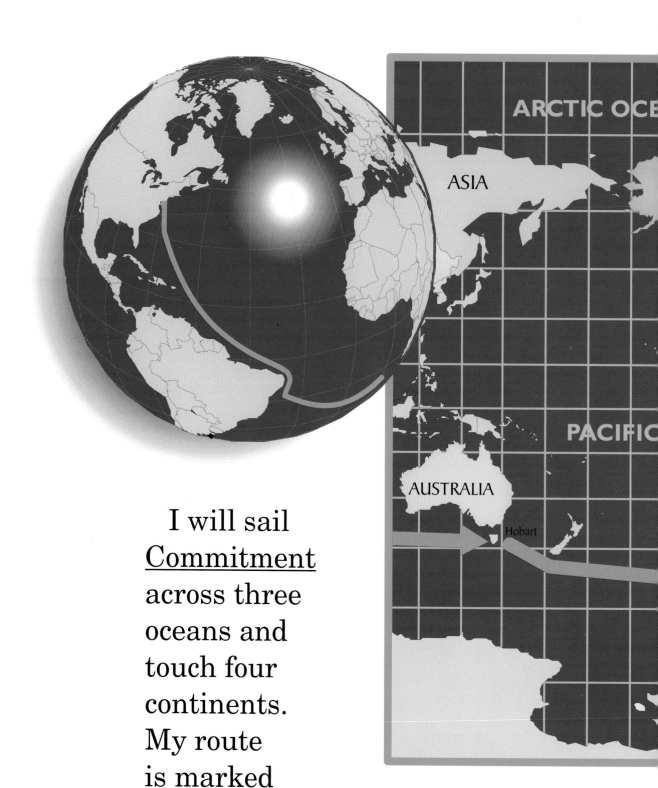

I will sail <u>Commitment</u> across three oceans and touch four continents. My route is marked in orange.

This flat map of the round earth shows all of Captain Bill's journey.

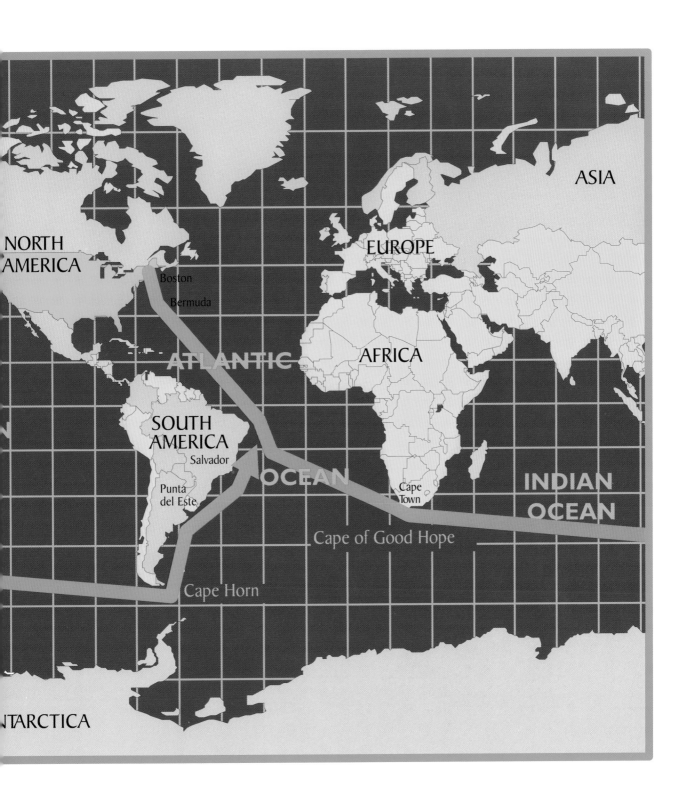

Charts are sea maps.
Many are shown later
in this book.

Captain Bill talks
to students by radio.

He cooks his meals
in the galley, the
kitchen of the boat.

Commitment is a snug home.
I do everything by myself.

On Wednesday nights Captain Bill watches videos.

Captain Bill sleeps in his bunk.

Day and night it sails along, even when I'm asleep.

On the way to Bermuda,
I meet a pilot whale
that is curious about
<u>Commitment</u> and me.

Whales are not fish.
They are big mammals
that swim to the
surface to breathe air.

12

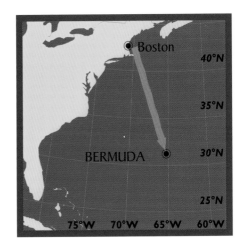

Houses on Bermuda have special roofs that collect rain for drinking and washing.

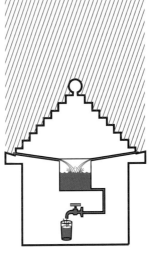

After sailing for eight days, I see land. It is the island of Bermuda, far out in the Atlantic Ocean.

Hooray! I am crossing the equator, the imaginary line between the northern and southern halves of the earth. Sailors always have a party when they "cross the line."

Northern Hemisphere

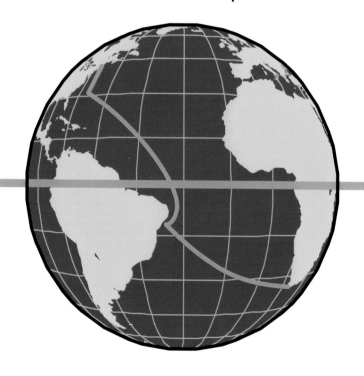

Equator

Southern Hemisphere

Like Captain Bill, many sailors have had
African ancestors.

Paul Cuffe
was a ship
owner
in Marion,
Massachusetts.

Absalom Boston was captain
of a whaling ship.
His sailors were
African Americans,
too.

Bill Pinkney
was a U.S. Navy
sailor for eight years.

Captain Michael Healy's ship
patrolled the icy coast of Alaska.

South America! In Salvador, Brazil, I meet children in a marching band, beating exciting rhythms on their drums.

Boston

BERMUDA

RAIN FOREST

0°

10°S

Salvador

B R A Z I L

20°S

PACIFIC
OCEAN

30°S

40°S

ATLANTIC
OCEAN

50°S

Macaws live high in the trees of the rain forest.

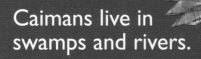

Caimans live in swamps and rivers.

The world's biggest rain forest is in South America.

His route will take him 32,000 miles!

Walking that far would take 1,067 days.

If a car could drive over water, it would take 36 days.

An airplane would take only 3 days.

<u>Commitment</u> will sail it in 259 days.

18

I use the radio to talk with students almost every day. The students are following my voyage on their maps.

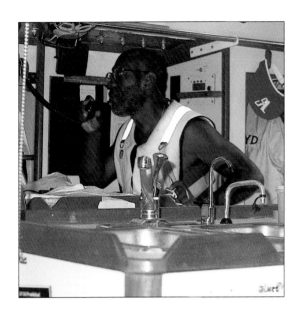

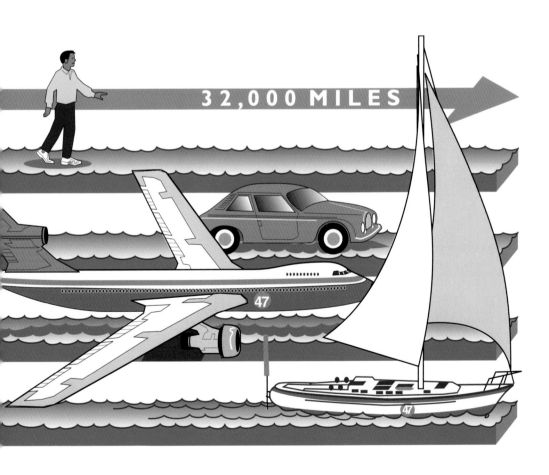

32,000 MILES

SOUTH
AMERICA

Salvador
BRAZIL

Thirty-four days after I leave Brazil, I sail into Cape Town, South Africa.

One hundred fifty years ago, my ancestors were taken from Africa in slave ships. Today slavery is against the law in almost every country.

40°W

30°W

AFRICA

The lion and the rhinoceros live in Africa.

Captain Bill makes new friends in South Africa.

SOUTH AFRICA
Cape Town

Cape of Good Hope

0°   10°E   20°E   30°E   **21**

Storm! Only eight days away from Cape Town, <u>Commitment</u> is rolling and pitching in strong winds and waves.

22

This is no fun! The waves are as tall as apartment buildings. I hold on tight and hope the storm ends soon.

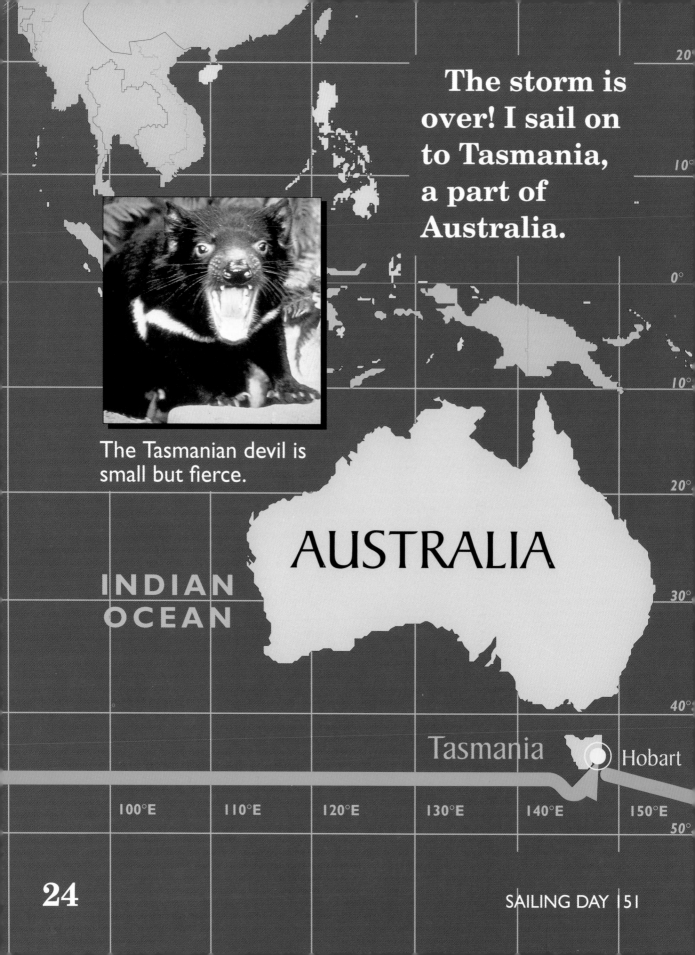

The storm is over! I sail on to Tasmania, a part of Australia.

The Tasmanian devil is small but fierce.

INDIAN OCEAN

AUSTRALIA

Tasmania

Hobart

20°

10°

0°

10°

20°

30°

40°

50°

100°E 110°E 120°E 130°E 140°E 150°E

The kangaroo bounces on its strong hind legs.

The koala lives in eucalyptus trees and almost never touches the ground.

The kookaburra's voice sounds like silly laughing.

The platypus has a duck bill and a beaver tail. It lays eggs like a bird.

NEW ZEALAND

170°E 180° 170°W 160°W 150°W 140°W

PACIFIC OCEAN

I leave Australia for the longest part of my trip— fifty-two days without seeing land!

A bird rests on <u>Commitment.</u>

A hawksbill turtle swims by.

I check my charts and listen to weather reports. Animals that live far from land are my only company.

White sharks live under the waves.

Cape Horn scares sailors. The winds howl, the waves are huge, and the weather is cold and rainy.

Soon I can turn north toward Boston, but now I need all my skills to survive.

Boston

BERMUDA

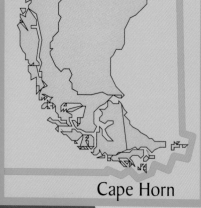

Cape Horn

Punta del Este
URUGUAY

PACIFIC
OCEAN

ATLANTIC
OCEAN

SAILING DAY 203

 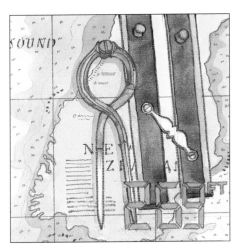

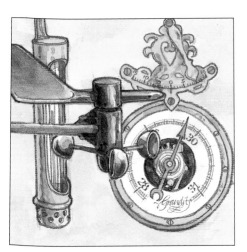 

To make this trip, Captain Bill had to study math, geography, and science. Reading, however, was his most important skill.

I made it! I have kept my promise. I have made my dream come true.

On the dock in Boston, some of
the students who were my radio
friends are waiting. I am so happy
to be back. I have so many stories
to share with them.

GLOSSARY

BUNK: A bed on a boat.

CAPE: A piece of land sticking out
  into the water.

CONTINENT: One of seven very large bodies
  of land on the earth.

CHART: An ocean map used by sailors.

HARBOR: A shelter along a coast that
  protects ships.

HEMISPHERE: Half of the earth.

ISLAND: A piece of land entirely surrounded
  by water.

OCEAN: A very large body of salt water.

RADAR (RAdio Detecting And Ranging): A radio
  device that helps ships and planes find their
  way at night or in bad weather.

ROUTE: The path from one place to another.

ROLL: To rock from side to side.

PITCH: To rock from front to back.

VOYAGE: A long trip.